I Can Cook!

FRENCH FOOD

Wendy
Blaxland

A⁺

Smart Apple Media
P.O. Box 3263
Mankato, MN, 56002

Reprinted 2012

First published in 2011 by
MACMILLAN EDUCATION AUSTRALIA PTY LTD
15–19 Claremont St, South Yarra, Australia 3141

Visit our website at www.macmillan.com.au or go directly to www.macmillanlibrary.com.au

Associated companies and representatives throughout the world.

Copyright text © Wendy Blaxland 2011

Library of Congress Cataloging-in-Publication Data

Blaxland, Wendy.
   French food / Wendy Blaxland.
      p. cm. — (I can cook!)
   Includes index.
   Summary:"Describes historical, cultural, and geographical factors that have influenced the cuisine of France.
   Includes recipes to create French food"—Provided by publisher.
   ISBN 978-1-59920-669-1 (library binding)
   1. Cooking, French—Juvenile literature. 2. Food—France—History—Juvenile literature. 3. Cookbooks. I. Title.
   TX719.B6424 2012
641.5944—dc22
                     2011005445

Publisher: Carmel Heron
Commissioning Editor: Niki Horin
Managing Editor: Vanessa Lanaway
Editor: Laura Jeanne Gobal
Proofreaders: Georgina Garner; Kirstie Innes–Will
Designer: Stella Vassiliou
Page Layout: Stella Vassiliou
Photo Researcher: Claire Armstrong (management: Debbie Gallagher)
Illustrators: Jacki Sosenko; Guy Holt (map, **7**, **9**); Gregory Baldwin (map icons, **9**)
Production Controller: Vanessa Johnson

Manufactured in China by Macmillan Production (Asia) Ltd.
Kwun Tong, Kowloon, Hong Kong
Supplier Code: CP March 2011

Acknowledgments
The author would like to thank the following for their generous help and expert advice: Emeritus Professor Eugene Anderson, University of California; Lynne Olver, editor, FoodTimeline; Professor Barbara Santich, University of Adelaide; and Dena Saulsbury-Monaco, cook and librarian, Montreal.

The author and the publisher are grateful to the following for permission to reproduce copyright material:

Front cover photographs: Grated carrots © Corbis/H et M; pancakes courtesy of iStockphoto.com/Douglas_Freer; omelette courtesy of iStockphoto.com/ Issaurinko; toasted ham & cheese sandwich courtesy of Shutterstock/Joe Gough; pomegranate juice courtesy of Shutterstock/Ivaschenko Roman.
Back cover photographs: Brown paper bag courtesy of Shutterstock/Nils Z; chocolate strawberries courtesy of Shutterstock/CURAphotography; mushrooms courtesy of Shutterstock/Ivaylo Ivanov; baguettes courtesy of Shutterstock/Maceofoto; garlic courtesy of Shutterstock/restyler; and artichokes courtesy of Shutterstock/Valentyn Volkov.

Photographs courtesy of: Corbis/Glowimages, **25** (top center), /H et M, **19** (carrot salad); Dreamstime/Astrug, **6** (croissant); Getty Images /Marie-Louise Avery, **15** (toasted sandwich), /James Baigrie, **17** (main omelette), /Eric Feferberg, **28**, /Winfried Heinze, **5**, /Lisa Linder, **21** (top left); iStockphoto.com/ajafoto, **10** (tea towel), /albertc111, **6** (travel stamps), /brinkstock, **13** (clipboard), /gbh007, **4** (girl), /gerisima, **6** (suitcase), /gojak, **20** (lemons), **21** (lemons), /Irochka_T, **25** (ice), /Jamesmcq24, **17** (green onions), /Robyn Mac, **10** (hanging utensils), /Urosh Petrovic, **throughout** (red oven mitt); Photolibrary/Alamy/© Farming Today, **6** (pain rustique), /Alamy/© Osb70, **29**, /Alamy/© Pick and Mix Images, **27**, /Alamy/© Robert Harding Picture Library Ltd, **7** (top right); PixMac/ Dana Krimmling, **7** (bottom left); Shutterstock/Ackab Photography, **7** (center left), /Afonkin_Y, **9** (rice), /Aaron Amat, **11** (grater), /Anat-oli, **9** (pig), /Petrenko Andriy, **8** (oats), /Mark Aplet, **13** (electric mixer), /Roxana Bashyrova, **26** (grapes), /Nikola Bilic, **16** (parsley), **17** (parsley), **19** (parsley), /bonchan, **30** (top), /Adrian Britton, **10** (baking tray), /Darren Brode, **11** (electric mixer), /buriy, **8** (rice), /Ilker Canikligil, **10** (saucepan), **13** (saucepan), /Norman Chan, **8** (clams), /ZH Chen, **10** (measuring cups), /Colour, **8** (chicken), /Coprid, **13** (soap dispenser), /Luis Francisco Cordero, **10** (whisk), /CURAphotography, **23** (top left), / Mikael Damkier, **10** (frying pan, measuring jug), /Raphael Daniaud, **11** (blender), /Ariadna De Raadt, **7** (center right), /Lulu Durand, **7** (top left), /ejwhite, **11** (colander), /Christopher Elwell, **8** (potatoes, watermelon), /Iakov Filimonov, **13** (knives), /Kellie L Folkerts, **8** (milk), /Gilmanshin, **13** (knife block), /GrigoryL, **14** (cheese), **15** (cheese), /Jiang Hongyan, **17** (eggs), **20** (eggs), **21** (eggs), /Tischenko Irina, **10** (large knife, butter knife), /Eric Isselée, **9** (cow, sheep), /Bernd Jürgens, **8** (pork), /K13 ART, **8** (blue bowl), **11** (bowls), /Kamira, **15** (bread), /Kayros Studio, **8** (fire extinguisher), /Vitaly Korovin, **6** (tomatoes), **8** (tomatoes), /LazarevDN, **10** (sieve), /Chris Leachman, **10** (chopping board), /Le Do, **8** (baguettes), /Maceofoto, **6** (baguette), /Petr Malyshev, **13** (kettle), **31**, /max777, **9** (chestnuts), /Marco Mayer, **7** (bottom right), **8** (barley), /Iain McGillivray, **10** (tongs), /Melica, **18** (carrots), **19** (carrots), /Monkey Business Images, **30** (center), /Mopic, **13** (first-aid box), /Nattika, **8** (eggplants), /odze, **22**, **23** (strawberries), **25** (pomegranate seeds), **26** (strawberries), /Zhuchkova Olena, **9** (oats), /M Unal Ozmen, **4** (chocolate), **23** (chocolate), /Paul Paladin, **8** (cheese wedges), /Photocrea, **8** (peas), /Tatiana Popova, **8** (round cheese), /Ragnarock, **11** (slotted spoon), **13** (frying pan), /Julián Rovagnati, **9** (fruit & veg), /Andrei Rybachuk, **24** (pomegranate), /Antonio S., **8** (mussels), **9** (mussels), /S1001, **8** (apples), /Sally Scott, **8** (strawberries), /Anna Sedneva, **8** (zucchinis), /Becky Stares, **9** (chicken), /Alex Staroseltsev, **8** (beef), **9** (crayfish), /Stephen Aaron Rees, **11** (wooden spoon), /soncerina, **10** (fork), /STILLFX, **10** (peeler), /Ev Thomas, **13** (fire blanket), /tomkai, **8** (herbs), **9** (herbs), /Matt Valentine, **10** (bread knife), /GraÃ§a Victoria, **13** (oven mitts), **13** (oven mitts), /Vlue, **10** (steak knife), /Valentyn Volkov, **8** (raspberries), **25** (pomegranates), /Lynn Watson, **30** (bottom), /Julian Weber, **4** (pastries), /Yasonya, **8** (pears), /Yellowj, **8** (lobster), /Feng Yu, **14** (mustard), **15** (mustard).

While every care has been taken to trace and acknowledge copyright, the publisher tenders their apologies for any accidental infringement where copyright has proved untraceable. They would be pleased to come to a suitable arrangement with the rightful owner in each case.

Contents

Glossary Words

When a word is printed in **bold**, it is explained in the Glossary on page 31.

Cooking Tips

Safety Warning

Ask an adult for help when you see this red oven mitt on a recipe.

How To

Cooking techniques are explained in small boxes with this handprint.

I Can Cook!

Cooking is a rewarding and lifelong skill. With some basic cooking knowledge, a little practice, and great recipes, you can cook entire meals! Cooking for your family and friends is a fun activity, and a mouthwatering meal can take you to places that you have never been. Are you ready to have fun cooking—and eating?

A World of Food

Every day, people all over the world cook delicious and **nutritious** meals. What they cook depends not only on the ingredients available to them, but also on their country's food **culture** or cooking style. A country's style of cooking is shaped over time by its culture, **economy**, **climate**, and the land itself.

Cook Your Way Around the World

You can explore the great cuisines of the world in your own kitchen. The special flavors and wonderful aromas of a country's food culture come from fresh ingredients and particular spices or herbs, which you can find in your local supermarket or a specialty store. Share with your family and friends authentic dishes from different countries that look great and taste even better.

You can cook mouthwatering food from different countries by following a few simple steps. Some recipes involve combining just a couple of ingredients!

French Food

Sharing meals is an important part of French culture. The French also place great importance on the way food looks. This means even a simple French picnic is a feast for the eyes as well as the tastebuds.

French Food Worldwide

Buttery croissants, crepes, and French fries are known worldwide, as are salads flavored with a sharp vinaigrette dressing and the tiny cakes called petits fours.

Eating the French Way

Fresh local and seasonal French ingredients are available at local markets and most people buy their meat and produce daily. Breakfast is simple—bread, jam, and coffee. Lunch used to be the main meal and families would return home for this. However, these days, particularly in cities, dinner is the main meal. Food styles vary widely from hearty peasant dishes to delicate fruit tarts and are also influenced by the cuisines of neighboring countries.

Cooking French Food At Home

It is surprisingly easy to create an authentic French meal at home. Sometimes all you need is good French bread, cheese and fruit! This book has seven recipes that you can follow to cook a meal on your own or with a little help from an adult. Some of the recipes don't even involve cooking. The recipes can be adapted to suit special **diets**, too.

NORTH AMERICA

FRANCE → EUROPE

ASIA

AFRICA

SOUTH AMERICA

AUSTRALIA

N ↑

France is found in Europe. It shares borders with eight countries.

A special French treat at breakfast is *pain au chocolat*, a sweet pastry with chocolate inside.

Traditions and Styles

France has a **tradition** of elegant dining based on food cooked for the upper classes centuries ago. It also has a variety of simple regional styles that emerged from food cooked daily in villages and on farms.

The French bake fresh bread twice daily and eat bread at every meal.

The Development of French Food

French food styles vary widely from region to region, depending on the history, economy, and climate of the region and the ingredients available during each season. Catherine de' Medici brought the Italian passion for fresh ingredients and fine dining with her when she became the French queen in 1533. Later, famous **chefs** wrote cookbooks that helped develop elaborate cooking styles for the rich. At the same time, simpler and distinctive cooking styles were being created regionally with local ingredients, often influenced by neighboring countries. This extended to cheese and wine as well, with every region having its own styles.

African Influence

France is home to many African **migrants** from its former **colonies**. They brought their own ingredients, cooking styles, and traditional dishes, many of which are now common in French cooking, including couscous.

Regional Food

The cooking style of each French region is based on what's in season and available locally. Some well-loved regional specialties have become popular all over France. The map below breaks France up into six main regions and discusses the ingredients and special foods that are popular in each.

Central

The **fertile** plains and rivers around Île-de-France provide vegetables, fruit, mushrooms, and the soft cheese known as Brie. In Burgundy, great wines led to the development of dishes such as beef bourguignon (beef cooked in wine) and coq au vin (chicken in wine, pictured). Escargots (cooked snails) are popular here, too, and Dijon mustard.

Northeast

Heavier food, such as cold meats and potato-based dishes, is commonly cooked in Alsace and Lorraine. Specialties include pastries and jams, as well as German-influenced pork dishes (pictured) and pickles.

Northwest

Normandy's apples and dairy products, such as butter, cream, and Camembert cheese (pictured), are used in rich tarts. Coastal waters supply fish, including trout and salmon, and other seafood, such as mussels and oysters. Brittany is known for its wide, thin pancakes called galettes.

Mideast

The mountainous parts of this region are famous for cheese, which may be used in fondues (pictured), and Lyon sausages.

Southwest

Aquitaine is famous for its saltwater and freshwater fish, and Bordeaux for its free-range poultry. Truffles and mushrooms are found on the high plains of Périgord. Well-known dishes here include cassoulet (pictured), a hearty bean stew from Toulouse.

Southeast

Cooks in this Mediterranean area use olive oil, garlic, anchovies, herbs, lavender, and honey. The region of Languedoc-Roussillon provides seafood and snails, as well as cheese and meat from both sheep and goats. Ratatouille (pictured), a well-known vegetable dish, comes from Provence, as does the fish stew bouillabaisse.

GERMANY

BELGIUM

LUXEMBOURG

NORTHEAST

NORTHWEST

CENTRAL

SWITZERLAND

MIDEAST

ITALY

SOUTHWEST

SOUTHEAST

Mediterranean Sea

SPAIN

ANDORRA

French Ingredients

Fresh seasonal produce is the foundation of any French meal. The key ingredients of French cooking come from the French land and the seas that surround it, and are sold in local markets, specialty stores, and supermarkets.

Meat
Hearty French dishes rely on meat, such as beef, pork, and chicken.

Seafood
Along the coasts, fish and other seafood, such as clams and lobsters, are popular.

Dairy Products
Milk and cheese are widely used in French cooking.

Fruit
Apples, peaches, and pears are popular, as are summer fruit, such as strawberries and raspberries. In the south, watermelons are often eaten.

Staple Foods
Bread is a **staple food** in France and is served with every meal. French bread is usually made from wheat, though buckwheat flour is also used. Barley, oats, and rice are also eaten.

Vegetables
Potatoes, tomatoes, peas, zucchini, and eggplants are popular in French cooking.

Landscapes and Climates

France's landscapes include mountainous areas, rocky coasts, and fertile plains watered by many rivers. The south of France has a warm, Mediterranean climate, while the north is **temperate**. The west coast has a milder climate. France's mountainous areas have cold winters. The map below shows which areas of the country France's produce comes from.

Apples

Normandy's climate lets it grow its famous apples, which are used in tarts, baked whole, or pressed for apple cider and vinegar.

Farmers raise cattle for beef through the center of France as well as in Normandy and Brittany.

Poultry farms are concentrated in the central and western areas.

Dairy products come from Normandy and pigs are mainly raised in Brittany.

UNITED KINGDOM

English Channel

BELGIUM

GERMANY

LUXEMBOURG

Chestnuts are grown in the southern and central forests, especially in the Ardèche.

NORTHEAST

NORTHWEST

CENTRAL

SWITZERLAND

Sheep are farmed in the south and on the island of Corsica.

Farmers grow wheat, corn, potatoes, and sugar beets in the north and around Paris. Barley, oats, canola, and sunflowers are grown on the central plains and in Brittany and Normandy.

MIDEAST

ITALY

Atlantic Ocean

Coastal waters of the Atlantic supply seafood, such as salmon, oysters, and mussels.

SOUTHWEST

SOUTHEAST

Fruit and vegetables come from the valleys of the Loire, Seine, Rhône, and Garonne rivers, as well as from the south around Perpignan, Marseille, and Nice.

SPAIN

ANDORRA

Mediterranean Sea

Herbs, such as oregano, thyme, and rosemary, are grown in the south.

Rice grows in the Camargue, an area in the south.

Tuna is caught and farmed in the coastal waters of the Mediterranean, which also supplies seafood, such as lobsters.

Cooking Basics

Equipment

Having the right equipment to cook with is very important. Here are some of the most common items needed in the kitchen.

Potato mashers break up food.

Sieves separate and break up food.

Spatulas lift and turn food.

Cook pasta, rice, soups, and stews in saucepans.

Big knives chop. Small knives cut and peel. Butter knives spread. Serrated knives slice.

Oven mitts protect hands from heat.

Baking pans hold food in an oven.

Forks hold, stir, or prick food.

Whisks beat food to add air and make it light.

Tongs are used to handle hot food.

Measuring cups and spoons measure ingredients accurately.

Frying pans fry or brown food.

Peelers remove the skins from fruit and vegetables.

Cutting boards provide safe surfaces for cutting food.

Blenders chop ingredients, mix food, and make smooth sauces and soups.

Spoons mix and stir. Wooden spoons prevent scratched pans. Slotted spoons let liquid drain away.

Graters shave thin slices from food, such as cheese.

Colanders drain liquids.

Mixers mix food quickly.

Bowls hold food for mixing.

Weight, Volume, Temperature, and Special Diets

It is important to use the right amount of ingredients, cook at the correct heat, and be aware of people with special dietary needs.

Weight and Volume

The weight and volume of ingredients can be measured with a weighing scale or with measuring cups and spoons. Convert them using this table. Measure dry ingredients so that they are level across the top of the spoon or cup without packing them down.

Recipe Measurement	Weight	Volume
1 cup	8 ounces	250 ml
½ cup	4 ounces	125 ml
2 tablespoons	1 ounce	30 ml
1 teaspoon	0.16 ounce	4.7 ml

Temperature

Fahrenheit and Celsius are two different ways of measuring temperature. Oven dials may show the temperature in either Fahrenheit or Celsius. Use lower temperatures in gas or convection ovens.

Oven Temperature	Celsius	Fahrenheit
Slow	150°	300°
Moderately slow	160°–170°	320°–340°
Moderate	180°	350°
Moderately hot	190°	375°
Hot	200°	400°
Very hot	220°–240°	430°–470°

Special Diets

Some people follow special diets because of personal or religious beliefs about what they should eat. Others must not eat certain foods because they are **allergic** to them.

Diet	What It Means	Symbol
Allergy-specific	Some people's bodies react to a certain food as if it were poison. They may die from eating even a tiny amount of this food. Nuts, eggs, milk, strawberries, and even chocolate may cause allergic reactions.	
Halal	**Muslims** eat only food prepared according to strict religious guidelines. This is called halal food.	
Kosher	**Jews** eat only food prepared according to strict religious guidelines. This is called kosher food.	
Vegan	Vegans eat nothing from animals, including dairy products, eggs, and honey.	
Vegetarian	Vegetarians eat no animal products and may or may not eat dairy products, eggs, and honey.	

Safety and Hygiene

Be safe in the kitchen by staying alert and using equipment correctly when cooking. Practicing good food hygiene means you always serve clean, germ-free food. Follow the handy tips below!

Be Organized

Hungry? Organized cooks eat sooner! First, read the recipe. Next, take out the equipment and ingredients you'll need and follow the stages set out in the recipe. Straighten up and clean as you go. While your food cooks, wash up, sweep the kitchen floor, and empty the garbage.

Heat

Place boiling saucepans toward the back of the stove with handles turned inward. Keep your hands and face away from steam and switch hot equipment off as soon as you have finished using it. Use oven mitts to pick up hot pots and put them down on heatproof surfaces. Always check that food is cool enough to eat.

Emergencies

All kitchens should have a fire blanket, fire extinguisher and first-aid box.

Food Hygiene

To avoid spreading germs, wash your hands well and keep coughs and sneezes away from food. Use fresh ingredients and always store food that spoils easily, such as meat and fish, in the refrigerator.

Electricity

Use electrical equipment only with an adult's help. Switch the power off before unplugging any equipment and keep it away from water.

Knives

When cutting food with a knife, cut away from yourself and onto a nonslip surface, such as a suitable cutting board.

Let's Cook!

MAKES: 2 sandwiches

PREPARATION TIME: 5 minutes

COOKING TIME: 5 minutes

FOOD VALUES: About 275 **calories**, 12 grams of fat, 12 grams of **protein**, and 29 grams of **carbohydrates** per sandwich.

SPECIAL DIETS: Suitable for nut-free diets. For vegan and vegetarian diets, use a vegetarian meat substitute, and vegans should use a soy-based cheese; for **gluten**-free diets, use gluten-free bread; and for kosher and halal diets, use a certified substitute for ham, such as chicken slices.

Croque Monsieur

Many cultures enjoy sandwiches spread or filled with tasty treats. This toasted ham and cheese sandwich is known all over France simply as a *croque,* or "crunchy." It is usually made with Emmentaler or Gruyère cheese and was first recorded in a Parisian menu in 1910.

Equipment

- Grater
- Butter knife
- Serving plate
- Frying pan
- Spatula

Ingredients

- Gruyère cheese (or your favorite)
- 4 slices of bread
- 1 tablespoon of Dijon mustard
- 2 slices of ham
- 1 tablespoon of margarine (or butter)

What to Do

1 Grate one cup of cheese.

2 Spread the mustard evenly on two slices of bread. Next, put one slice of ham on each slice, on top of the mustard.

3 Sprinkle half a cup of cheese over each slice of ham.

Recipe Variations

Top the sandwich with a fried egg to make a *croque madame*.

Instead of sandwich bread, use a fresh croissant (a crescent-shaped French pastry), fill it with ham and grated cheese, and heat it.

Ask an adult for help with using the stove.

4

Top the ham with the remaining slices of bread to form two sandwiches. Next, spread the margarine on the outside of the sandwiches.

5

Cook the sandwiches in the frying pan until they turn golden brown (about 2–3 minutes).

6

Use a spatula to turn the sandwiches over. Cook them until the other side turns golden brown, too (about 2 minutes). Serve immediately.

15

Omelette

The original inspiration for the omelette was a recipe for cooked beaten eggs from Persia (modern-day Iran). Since the 1500s, omelettes have been a French favorite. They are cooked quickly in a small frying pan with sizzling butter and eaten piping hot with fresh, crusty bread and a green salad.

MAKES: 1 omelette

PREPARATION TIME: 10 minutes

COOKING TIME: 2 minutes

FOOD VALUES: About 170 calories, 8 g of fat, 3 g of protein, and 1 g of carbohydrates per omelette.

SPECIAL DIETS: Suitable for vegetarian, gluten-free, nut-free, kosher, and halal diets. Not suitable for vegan diets.

Recipe Variations

Make a heartier meal by adding tomatoes and cooked diced vegetables to the omelette as it begins to set. Turn the heat down to cook the omelette a little more slowly.

Equipment

- Mixing bowl
- Fork
- Heavy, small frying pan
- Spatula
- Serving plate

Ingredients

- 2 eggs
- 1 tablespoon of milk (optional)
- Salt and pepper, to taste
- 1 teaspoon of vegetable oil (canola or sunflower)
- A few sprigs of fresh parsley (or scallions), chopped finely

What to Do

1

Break the eggs into the bowl. Add the milk, salt, and pepper, and **beat** the mixture with the fork until combined.

2

Heat the frying pan on medium to high heat until you can feel the heat rising from it when you hold your hand above the pan. Add the oil to the pan.

3

Pour the egg mixture into the pan. Let the mixture bubble and set without stirring for about 30 seconds.

How To: Beat

Mix the eggs, milk, salt and pepper very quickly with the fork until they are completely combined.

Ask an adult for help with using the stove.

4

Use the spatula to pull the cooked mixture from the sides of the pan toward the center. Tilt the pan to let the uncooked mixture spread and cook.

5

Sprinkle the parsley onto the omelette.

6

When the top of the omelette has set, take the pan off the stove. Loosen the omelette carefully with the spatula and tip it onto the serving plate, folding the side over to make a half-moon shape as you do so. Serve immediately.

Let's Cook!

Carrot Salad

Most French main meals include a delicious, colorful salad dressed with a vinaigrette made from oil (often olive oil) and vinegar or lemon juice, sometimes with a hint of garlic. This grated carrot salad is so popular in France that it is available in almost every delicatessen.

MAKES: 2 servings

PREPARATION TIME: 10 minutes

FOOD VALUES: About 45 calories, 3 g of fat, 1 g of protein, and 6 g of carbohydrates per serving.

SPECIAL DIETS: Suitable for vegan, vegetarian, nut-free, gluten-free, kosher, and halal diets.

Recipe Variations

Add halved orange segments and replace half of the lemon juice with orange juice for a different flavor.

Replace the parsley with chopped mixed herbs, such as basil and thyme.

Equipment

- Cutting board
- Small, sharp knife
- Grater
- Serving bowl
- Screw-top jar
- Salad servers

Ingredients

- 2 medium-size carrots
- 3 stems of fresh parsley
- 1 tablespoon of olive oil
- ½ tablespoon of lemon juice
- Salt and pepper, to taste

What to Do

1 Wash the carrots. Cut the ends off and throw them away. Grate the carrots finely into the bowl.

2 Chop the parsley finely, then add it to the grated carrots.

Ask an adult for help with using the knife.

3 Add the olive oil, lemon juice, salt, and pepper to the screw-top jar. Close it and shake the ingredients until thoroughly mixed.

4 Drizzle the dressing onto the grated carrots and parsley.

5 Toss the salad well with the salad servers so that the vinaigrette is thoroughly mixed in, and serve.

Makes: 8 small crepes

Preparation time: 40 minutes

Cooking time: 15 minutes

Food values: About 65 calories, 2 g of fat, 3 g of protein, and 10 g of carbohydrates per crepe.

Special diets: Suitable for vegetarian and nut-free diets. Not suitable for vegan diets. For gluten-free diets, use gluten-free flour; and for kosher and halal diets, replace ham with other certified meat.

Mini-crepes

Crepes are thin, light French pancakes served with either sweet or savory fillings. Though they are popular all year, families traditionally make them during the **Catholic** festival of Candlemas (February 2). In Brittany, huge, paper-thin crepes called "galettes," made of buckwheat flour, are cooked on enormous iron plates, often at street stands.

Equipment

- Bowl
- Fork
- Fine mesh sieve
- Wooden spoon
- Frying pan
- Tablespoon
- Spatula
- 2 serving plates
- Teaspoon

Ingredients

- 1 large egg
- ½ cup of plain flour
- ½ cup of milk
- 1 teaspoon of margarine (or butter)
- ½ cup of powdered sugar
- 1 lemon, cut into wedges

What to Do

1 Break the egg into the bowl and **beat** it lightly with the fork.

2 Sieve half of the flour into the beaten egg. Mix it in well. Next, sieve the rest of the flour in and stir until a smooth paste forms.

3 Gradually add the milk and stir until the batter is smooth. It should be thin enough to pour. Add a little more milk if necessary. Check that the batter has no lumps. Tap the bowl gently on the counter to get rid of bubbles. Let the batter rest for 30 minutes.

How To: Beat

Mix the egg very quickly with the fork.

Recipe Variations

Instead of lemon juice and sugar, use a chocolate and hazelnut spread on the crepes.

Fill the crepes with tomato, mozzarella, olive oil, and capers for a Provençal touch instead of using sugar and lemon juice.

Ask an adult for help with using the stove.

4 Lightly grease the frying pan with a little margarine and heat the pan over medium heat. When the pan is hot, pour 1 tablespoon of batter into the pan and quickly swirl it to create a circle about 3½ inches in diameter.

5 Cook until the top of the crepe does not look wet and shiny (about 1 minute), then loosen the edges of the crepe and flip it with a spatula onto the other side. Cook until the crepe starts to brown a little (about 30 seconds).

6 Transfer the crepe to the plate. If this first crepe is not thin enough, add a little more milk to the batter. Repeat steps 4–6 until all of the batter has been used.

7 Sprinkle a teaspoon of powdered sugar across the center of each crepe, and squeeze juice from a lemon wedge on top of this. Next, fold the crepe in half. Enjoy!

Chocolate-dipped Strawberries

Garden strawberries were first bred in Brittany around 1740. In this recipe, they are dipped in chocolate. This is a variation of the cooking style called fondue, which is common in France as well as other countries, where ingredients are dipped in a thick sauce.

MAKES: 12 strawberries (3 servings)

PREPARATION TIME: 15 minutes

COOKING TIME: 10 minutes

FOOD VALUES: About 175 calories, 9 g of fat, 3 g of protein, and 24 g of carbohydrates per serving.

SPECIAL DIETS: Suitable for vegetarian, nut-free, gluten-free, kosher, and halal diets. For vegan diets, use dark chocolate.

Equipment

- Saucepan large enough to hold bowl
- Medium-size metal bowl
- Serving plate, laid with parchment paper

Ingredients

- ½ pound of good chocolate chips or **couverture chocolate** (milk, dark, or white)
- 12 large fresh strawberries with leaves and stalks left on, washed and dried well

What to Do

1 Fill the saucepan ⅓ full with water. Bring the water to a boil, then turn down the heat to let the water simmer.

2 Put the chocolate in the bowl, then place the bowl in the saucepan. The hot water will melt the chocolate. Don't let any water enter the bowl or the chocolate will "seize" and become grainy.

3 Hold a strawberry by its stem and dip it halfway in the melted chocolate.

Recipe Variations

Create a pattern by dipping the strawberries in two kinds of chocolate, such as dark and white. Dip them first in one chocolate. When the chocolate has hardened, dip them again in the other chocolate halfway so you can see both kinds of chocolate.

Instead of strawberries, try dipping other fruit, such as grapes or cherries.

Ask an adult for help with using the stove.

4

Twirl the strawberry by its stem to shake off any excess chocolate and to avoid drips.

5

Set the strawberry on the plate. Repeat steps 3–5 with the remaining strawberries.

6

Let the chocolate on the strawberries cool and harden. You can also refrigerate them to speed up the process.

23

Let's Cook!

MAKES: 3 cups of grenadine syrup

PREPARATION TIME: 15 minutes

COOKING TIME: 15 minutes

FOOD VALUES: About 90 calories and 22 g of carbohydrates per glass. No fat or protein.

SPECIAL DIETS: Suitable for vegan, vegetarian, nut-free, gluten-free, kosher, and halal diets.

Recipe Variations

Add grenadine syrup to a glass of milk to make *bébé rose* (pink baby).

Add a little syrup to a glass of lemonade.

Grenadine

Grenadine is a tall, cool drink popular in France during summer, particularly in the south. Its name comes from "grenade," the French word for pomegranate, and it is made by diluting pomegranate syrup with water. Pomegranates are available during the fall and winter.

Equipment

- Cutting board
- Small, sharp knife
- Medium-size saucepan
- Wooden spoon
- 25-fluid-ounce glass bottle with cap
- Large saucepan
- Oven mitts
- Funnel
- Tablespoon
- 1 glass

Ingredients

- 6½ pounds of firm, ripe pomegranates
- 1 cup of sugar

What to Do

1 Gently roll a pomegranate on the cutting board with the heel of your hand to lightly crush the juice sacs around the seeds. Carefully make a small hole in the pomegranate and drain out as much juice as possible into the smaller saucepan. Repeat this step with each pomegranate.

2 Put the saucepan on the stove and stir the sugar into the juice over low heat to dissolve it.

3 Increase the heat until the syrup boils gently. Let it boil without stirring it until the syrup thickens slightly (about 15 minutes).

Ask an adult for help with using the knife and stove.

4

While the syrup is boiling, wash the bottle in hot, soapy water. Next, place it in the large saucepan, cover it with water, and boil it for 10 minutes. Ask an adult to drain the water from the saucepan, then remove the bottle from the saucepan while using a pair of oven mitts. Put it upside down to dry.

5

Using the funnel, pour the syrup into the clean, dry bottle and put the cap on immediately. The syrup can be stored for up to 2 months if left unopened in a cool, dark place. Open, it will keep in the refrigerator for a week.

6

To serve, pour 1 tablespoon of syrup into a glass and fill with cold water. Taste and add more syrup if necessary. Add ice if you wish.

A French Picnic

After the French Revolution (1789–99), during which King Louis XVI was overthrown, ordinary people were allowed into the royal parks for the first time. Having a picnic there became very popular. On Bastille Day in 2000, France celebrated with a 600-mile-long picnic from coast to coast. Traditional French picnics include bread, cheese, and fruit.

Serves: 4 people

Preparation time: 20 minutes

Food values: About 345 calories, 8 g fat, 16 g of protein, and 60 g of carbohydrates per serving.

Special diets: Suitable for nut-free diets. For vegan diets, avoid the cheese and ham; for vegetarian diets, avoid the ham; for gluten-free diets, use gluten-free bread; for kosher and halal diets, replace the ham with other certified meat.

Recipe Variations

Replace the baguette, ham, and cheese with sandwiches made the night before. Use your choice of ingredients!

Instead of strawberries and grapes, pack an apple tart, which you can get from a bakery.

Equipment

- 2 resealable storage bags
- 3 firm storage containers
- Insulated cooler
- Sharp knife
- 4 napkins
- Garbage bag
- 4 plates
- 4 cups
- Cutting board
- Picnic basket (or bag)
- Blanket

Ingredients

- 4 dill pickles
- 12 olives
- 2 fresh tomatoes or 12 cherry tomatoes, washed and dried
- 8 fresh lettuce leaves, washed and dried
- 1 pound of strawberries and grapes, washed and dried
- French cheese (Brie or Emmentaler)
- 4 slices of fresh ham or other delicatessen meat
- 1 large bottle of non-alcoholic apple cider
- Frozen bottle of water
- 1 fresh baguette or other French bread

What to Do

1

Store the pickles and olives in individual resealable bags and put these bags in one storage container. Next, pack the tomatoes, lettuce leaves, strawberries, and grapes in another container to avoid squashing them. Pack the cheese and ham in the third container.

2

Place the containers in the insulated cooler with the apple cider and frozen bottle of water to keep them cool.

3 Wrap the knife in the napkins, then pack it along with the garbage bag, plates, cups, and cutting board in the picnic basket. Place the blanket and bread on top.

4 Take the picnic basket and insulated cooler to your favorite picnic spot.

5 Spread the blanket on the ground and set up the food and drinks to share.

A French Food Celebration: Bastille Day

Bastille Day is a French national holiday celebrating the birth of France as a nation. On this day, French people enjoy special parades, street parties, and, of course, good French food.

What Is Bastille Day?

Bastille Day falls on July 14. It was first celebrated in 1790 to mark the first anniversary of the storming of a grim prison in Paris called the Bastille. People were often imprisoned here unfairly. Freeing these people began a revolution that led eventually to a new form of government, aiming to make all French citizens free, equal, and united.

How Is Bastille Day Celebrated?

Bastille Day begins with a military parade in Paris. This is the oldest and largest military parade in the world. Many people watch the parade on television. The French also celebrate Bastille Day with picnics and outdoor concerts, often dressed in the national colors of red, white, and blue.

Crowds watch as the Bastille Day military parade travels down the Champs-Elysées from the Arc de Triomphe.

Food

On Bastille Day, the French people often honor the revolution's heroes, who were peasants, with a simple picnic. Country villages and towns may celebrate with music, dancing, and a large outdoor meal for everyone. People may also celebrate privately, eating crepes or croissants for breakfast and having a long lunch of steak and chips. Their meal may end with delicious French pastries, tarts, or even macaroons (sweet cookies) in red, white, and blue.

Bastille Day Celebrations Worldwide

During the French revolution, the chefs who had fed the rich and the royals fled the country and set up their own restaurants. Today, chefs worldwide often prepare distinctively French food on Bastille Day. Dishes range from *gougères* (delicate cheese puffs) to main dishes of lobster and lamb, and *tarte tatin* (caramelized apple tart) for dessert.

Everyone enjoys themselves at traditional Bastille Day picnics when the weather is fine.

Try this!

Cooking is a creative skill you can enjoy every day. Try these activities and learn more about cooking French food.

- Find a recipe for soufflé, a baked egg dish. Amaze your friends by making this really easy treat.

- The French cook with really fresh food. Try growing your own vegetables so you always have a supply of fresh produce.

- Celebrate Bastille Day by cooking a French meal and decorating the table in red, white, and blue, France's national colors.

- Have you tried frogs' legs or snails? Look for recipes and dare to try them. How would you describe the taste?

- The French love apples. How many French recipes using apples can you collect? Pick your favorite recipe and make it.

- The delicate cakes and pastries in a French patisserie, or bakery, are almost too beautiful to eat. Visit one, pick your favorite cake or pastry, and look for a recipe so you can make it at home.

- Find out about the region of Provence. Enjoy a Provençal picnic featuring olives, cheese, shaved ham, and tapenade, a spread made from chopped olives, capers, and anchovies.

- Petits fours are tiny French cakes meant for afternoon tea, sometimes topped with icing flavored with lavender or orange. Ask an adult to take you to a French patisserie for your next birthday treat!

Glossary

allergic
having an allergy, or a bad reaction to certain foods

calories
units measuring the amount of energy food provides

carbohydrates
substances that provide the body with energy

Catholic
relating to the religion of Catholicism

chefs
skilled and trained cooks

climate
the general weather conditions of an area

colonies
countries or areas controlled by another country

***couverture* chocolate**
high-quality chocolate with extra cocoa butter, making it suitable for dipping

culture
the ways of living that a group of people has developed over time

diets
foods and drinks normally consumed by different people or groups of people

economy
the system of trade by which a country makes and uses its wealth

fertile
capable of producing good crops

gluten
a protein found in wheat and some other grains that makes dough springy

Jews
people who follow the religion of Judaism

migrants
people who move from one country to another to live permanently

Muslims
people who follow the religion of Islam

nutritious
providing nutrients, or nourishment

protein
a nutrient that helps bodies grow and heal

staple food
a food that is eaten regularly and is one of the main parts of a diet

temperate
a moderate climate without extreme temperatures

tradition
pattern of behavior handed down through generations

Index